THE KIDS' CAT BOOK

Owl Books are published by Greey de Pencier Books,
179 John Street, Suite 500, Toronto, ON M5T 3G5

The Owl colophon is a trademark of Owl Children's
Trust Inc. Greey de Pencier Books is a licensed user of
trademarks of Owl Children's Trust Inc.

Distributed in the U. S. by Firefly Books (U.S.) Inc.,
230 Fifth Ave., Suite 1607, New York, NY 10001

This book was published with the generous support of the
Canada Council and the Ontario Arts Council.

Special thanks to Dr. Gary Landsberg for his extensive assistance
on the revised edition.

Cataloguing in Publication Data
Main Entry under title:
The Kids cat book

Rev. ed.
ISBN 0-920775-51-9

1. Cats – juvenile literature.
I. Dingwall, Laima, 1953–   .
II. Slaight, Annabel, 1940–   .

SF445.7.K52 1990   599.74'428   C90-090063-6

Cover Design: Wycliffe Smith, Gary Beelik
Cover Photo: G J Images/The Image Bank Canada
Text Design: Nick Milton

Printed in Hong Kong

THE KIDS' CAT BOOK

From the Editors of OWL Magazine

CONTENTS

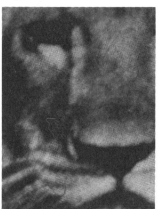

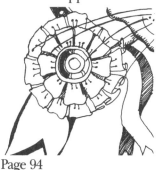

LOVE THAT CAT

Believe it or not, a cat is watching every one of these words being written. Cats are like that. They look after their own interests, and my cat, Rutherford, is letting me know she wants her picture in this book. Well okay, Rutherford, here's a nice drawing of you. Now, let's get this book under way!

Welcome to a book of amazing facts about domestic and wild cats with lots of stories and tips for understanding one of the world's most misunderstood creatures. This book has been created in response to questions sent in by the readers of OWL, the Discovery Magazine for Children. Scientists and veterinarians, even cat psychologists, have helped pull together the latest information.

This is a reference book and a fun book. We begin with some funny comments from real kids about why they love their cats. Do you suppose their cats supervised what they wrote, too?

Annabel Slaight

I love my cat Sonny because he's cute. He pounces on my sister (and he sometimes sleeps with her, too). But he always lets me scratch under his chin.
Barbara Janicek

My cat is the biggest cat in the world. He is bigger than my neighbor's dog. I don't love my cat because he's big, I love him because he's mine.
Bentley Forrest, 11

I love my cat Gusky. He is soft, bouncy and lovable. He sleeps on my bed.
Erin Hansen, 6

I love my cat because he gives me leg rubs and licks me for kisses. He is so nice.
Jennifer Mitchell, 10

Our tomcat Smokey is really sweet. Sometimes he's mean but he acts like he is human. I love him a lot.
Tracy Schiemann, 10

My two Siamese cats, Fatso and Molly, are lovable, cuddly and playful. They like to play with feet and elastics. They watch birds through the window. And they dance, too!
Kathleen Ovens, 9

My cat Sandy is cute. She fetches pom-poms and eats chocolate. Sometimes she rolls onto her back wanting a tummy rub.
Meagan Klaassen, 9

THE CAT UP CLOSE

Sometimes you get the feeling that your friendly little house cat thinks it's a big, ferocious tiger. That's not too surprising—after all, they're very close relatives.

Tail End

Most cats have a long tail containing 20 bones or more. This tail, an extension of the cat's spinal column (so please don't step on it), can be curled around a cat's feet to keep them warm or held out for balance while running and jumping. A cat's tail can also send messages. Watch it, and you can instantly learn whether a cat is happy, angry or frightened.

Graceful

Even the smallest cat has more bones than you do; 245 compared to your 206. So in the same way that a puppet with many joints moves more easily than one with fewer joints, a cat can put its body in more positions and is more agile than a human being.

Sharp Claws

There are five needle-sharp claws on each front foot and four on the back (though some cats may have two to four extra toes). They are important for climbing away from enemies, gripping, digging, hunting and fighting. Cats keep their claws in top condition by scratching trees, posts and even furniture.

Tippy-Toes

Cat's can run quickly and quietly by moving on their tiptoes. And when they jump, the pads on the bottom of their paws act like spongy slippers for soft, safe landings.

Pussyfooting

A cat stays cool by panting and by perspiring through its sweat glands located in the pads on the bottom of its paws. On hot days or when a cat is frightened, it can perspire so much that it leaves a trail of paw prints.

Small Shoulders

A cat has narrow shoulders and a tiny collarbone. This means a cat can keep its front legs close together to walk along narrow ledges or squeeze through small openings.

Raincoat

A cat's fur, consisting of large guard hairs and shorter underfur, protects its body from bites, scratches and hot and cold temperatures. Each guard hair is attached to a muscle that makes it stand on end whenever the cat is angry or alarmed. And because this is so startling to see, it is a very good scare tactic indeed.

Hold That Pose

How long can you crouch in one position without moving? Probably not as long as your cat. A cat's muscles are designed to let it "freeze" for long periods of time without getting tired. That's especially important when stalking prey.

Disappearing Act

Because cats need to walk softly, run swiftly and spring high into the air, all (except the cheetah) can pull in their needlelike claws alongside the bones at the end of their toes. When they are retracted, the claws slide into pockets. This way the claws are off the ground and out of the way.

Strong Legs

The muscles in a cat's legs are very strong, and built for jumping, sprinting and climbing.

EYES

Look-Ahead Eyes

Cats can't see too well close up, but they can judge long distances very accurately. Because a cat's eyes face forward, what each eye sees overlaps, giving a cat "stereo" vision just like yours. Although cats can move their eyes from side to side, they usually turn their heads to see. Why? Because, with front-facing eyes, it makes focusing easier.

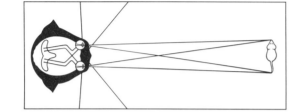

The Eye of the Cat

Why are cats' eyes so distinctive? It's because their pupils aren't always round like ours. A cat's pupils can close to tiny slits in bright sunlight, but open extra wide at night to let in as much light as possible.

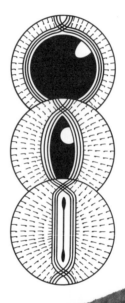

Sparkling Eyes

Flash a light into a cat's eyes and you'd swear that there are mirrors inside. In a way that's right, because at the back of each eye is a layer of shiny cells that catch and magnify any light coming in. These cells help cats see well to hunt at dusk or by moonlight.

Goggles

Cats, like many animals, have a special "third" eyelid next to the eye. This keeps the eye safe from dust and properly lubricated.

Color My World

Scientists used to think that cats could only see in black and white. But then they discovered that a cat's eyes, like yours, contain 'cones'— parts of the eye that detect color. Scientists are not sure what colors a cat sees, but they do know it sees fewer than you.

NOSE

Funny Face Flehmen

Have you ever seen a cat make a funny face as if it just tasted something odd? Then you have probably seen flehmen, or lip-curl behaviour. Around mating time a male cat will do this to test whether or not it likes a certain odor, especially those of female cats, by pressing its tongue against its vomeronasal organ (f), a small pouch in the roof of its mouth.

Nose Patch

The leatherlike nose pad you see on a cat is a protective covering for its very sensitive smelling apparatus.

Odor Sniffer

Have you ever noticed a cat lower and then quickly raise its nose away from a piece of just-cooked meat? Mainly, it's detecting odor, which is the principal deciding factor of whether it will eat the food or not. As the cat's nose is sensitive to hot and cold, as well, it can also tell whether the food is too hot to eat.

What a Smell

What is it about catnip that drives some cats crazy with delight? The smell. In fact, a mere whiff of this weed can send some cats rolling around in pure ecstasy. But not all cats like catnip. Scientists aren't sure why. How does your cat react to catnip?

Good Nose

Like all meat-eating animals, cats have a good sense of smell. And like all mammals, their main smell pathway is through the nose. The smell is then identified in the olfactory bulb (d) which is a part of the brain. A cat's sense of smell is much more sensitive than ours, but not nearly as strong as a dog's.

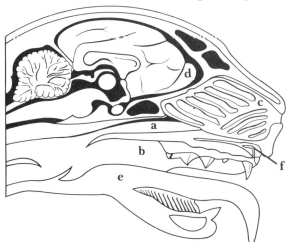

a) Nasal passage
b) Mouth
c) Smell cells
d) Olfactory bulb
e) Taste cells
f) Vomeronasal organ

EARS AND MORE

By Gum
Kittens are born without teeth. At about two weeks the baby or "milk" teeth start to come in. And it won't be until they are about six months old that they will have their full set of 30 teeth.

What Nice Chompers
Cats' teeth are excellent for biting but not grinding food. And because they cannot move their jaws sideways to chew like you can, they must swallow their food in small chunks.

A Comb with Teeth
A cat will sometimes use its teeth as a comb to get rid of knotted hair or clumps of dirt caught in its coat.

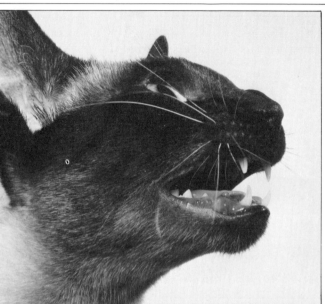

Accurate Bite
When a hunting cat catches a mouse, it can bite through the neck and sever the spinal cord without breaking any bones. How can it bite so accurately? Scientists think it might be helped by sensitive nerves at the base of each of its four canine teeth. These nerves probably sense where the bones are and, hence, the cat knows where not to bite down.

Swivel Ears
Cup your hands behind your ears and you'll understand why cats can hear so well. But it's not only the funnel shape of a cat's ears that helps it to pick up sound. Every cat has about 20 muscles in each ear so it can swivel them in almost any direction. Watch a cat do this while hunting. It's listening to every squeak and rustle, including some you can't hear at all.

Prickly Tongue

A lick from a tabby is like being rubbed by sandpaper, but the flick of a tiger's tongue could tear your skin. All cats have comblike spikes called papillae on their tongues that they use for brushing their fur and scraping meat from bones. When a cat drinks, its papillae trap liquid on its tongue. The larger the cat, the bigger and rougher the papillae.

Built-In Spoon

A cat can curl up the edges of its long, thin tongue to make a spoon—the better to lap up milk.

Sweet Soap

Some scientists think that a cat has a special ingredient —almost like a natural detergent—in its saliva. That may be one reason why a cat's fur smells so fresh, especially after grooming.

Sensitive Feelers

The stiff, wiry whiskers sticking out over a cat's eyes and from the sides of its face, are sensitive feelers. Even the slightest touch of these whiskers sends a message to the cat's brain. Thus a cat, by experience, learns that if it can squeeze its head through a narrow opening without its whiskers being touched, the rest of its body will probably be able to get through, too.

Look closely at the row of whiskers on the upper lip of this cat. Can you see a series of spots? One scientist studying lions found that each lion has a unique pattern of whisker spots—as individual as your finger-prints. If this is true for lions, scientists wonder if it's true for all cats.
What do you think?

CAT JOKES

Q. Why did the cat join the Red Cross?
A. It wanted to be a first aid kit.

Q. What cat can you never trust?
A. Cheetah.

Q. What do cats read?
A. Mewspapers.

Q. What did the leopard say when it started to rain?
A. That hits the spots.

Q. What do you get when you cross a lemon and a cat?
A. A sourpuss.

Q. What did the cat say as it ran through the screen door?
A. I feel strained.

Q. What makes more noise than a cat stuck in a tree?
A. Two cats stuck in a tree.

Q. Where do cats buy clothes?
A. From cat-alogues.

Q. What does a cat use to groom itself?
A. A catacomb.

Q. Why does a cat scratch itself?
A. It's the only one that knows where it itches.

Q. What's the difference between a cat and a comma?
A. A cat has claws at the end of its paws, but a comma is a pause at the end of a clause.

Q. What kind of cat says, "Woof, woof?"
A. A cat learning a foreign language.

DID YOU KNOW?

Cats sleep about half of their lives—that's twice as much as we humans, but the same as most other animals.

Each cat's nose pad is unique, like human fingerprints—no two cat noseprints are alike.

Lap, lap, lap, lap—swallow! When drinking, a cat laps four or five times with its tongue before each swallow.

Domestic cats usually have four to six kittens in one litter. But a record-holding Persian named Bluebell surprised everyone with 14 live kittens in her litter born in December, 1974.

If you've seen one leopard, then you haven't seen them all. That's because each leopard has a unique pattern of spots on its coat.

Do cats wash themselves just to keep clean? Not always. Sometimes cats wash when they are nervous, annoyed or anxious. It's a tension-relieving behavior, rather like you fiddling with your hair or clothes in awkward situations.

That tuft of hair at the end of a lion's tail hides a spur (a prickle, like in a rosebush). Scientists aren't sure what lions use this spur for, but—ouch—don't touch it, it's sharp.

If your cat falls from a high spot, it will probably land on its feet. All cats share this ability to right themselves. But no cat likes to be dropped, so please don't experiment. In fact, the impact of a fall from a great height may seriously injure a cat's legs or jaw. Quincy, a curious cat that slipped from a 19th-floor balcony, could confirm this. Amazingly enough he only broke one leg. Most cats would have suffered far worse.

FAMOUS CATS

If there were a Cat Hall of Fame, here are just a few famous felines you would see there. The tour begins with a 4,000-year-old...

Ancient Egyptians so admired cats that they mummified them when they died along with a few mice for food in the afterworld.

Lewis Carroll's tree-dwelling Cheshire cat in *Alice's Adventures in Wonderland* is so famous that we still use the expression "Cheshire grin" to describe someone's odd smile.

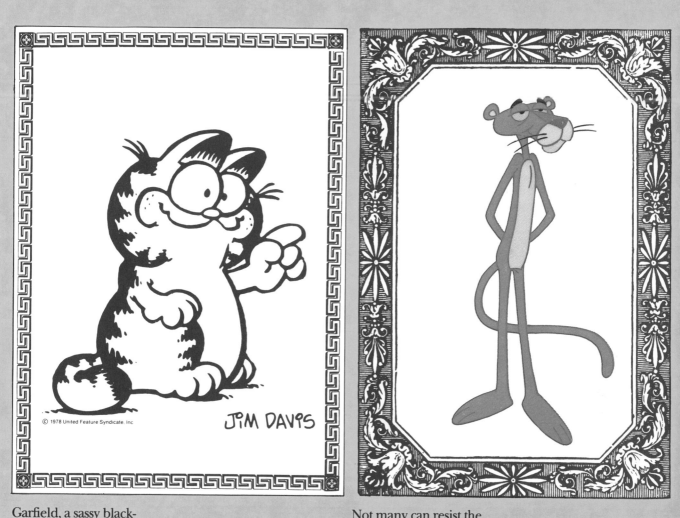

Garfield, a sassy black-striped marmalade created by Jim Davis, probably has become one of the best-loved cats of the 1980's.

Not many can resist the charms of the Pink Panther.

In the 14th century a penniless orphan, Dick Whittington, became Lord Mayor of London. His cat, so the story goes, made him rich by ridding a Moroccan king's castle of rats.

© 1978 United Feature Syndicate, Inc.

JIM DAVIS

Can your cat outwit a king or trick an ogre? Puss in Boots, of 17th-century fairy-tale fame, could.

When the Owl and the Pussycat went to sea in a beautiful pea-green boat, who would have imagined that they would eventually be married? But anything's possible in an Edward Lear 19th-century nonsense verse.

MGM's cat and mouse team, Tom and Jerry, quickly rose to stardom in the 1940's and won their creators—William Hanna and Joe Barbara—many Academy Award nominations.

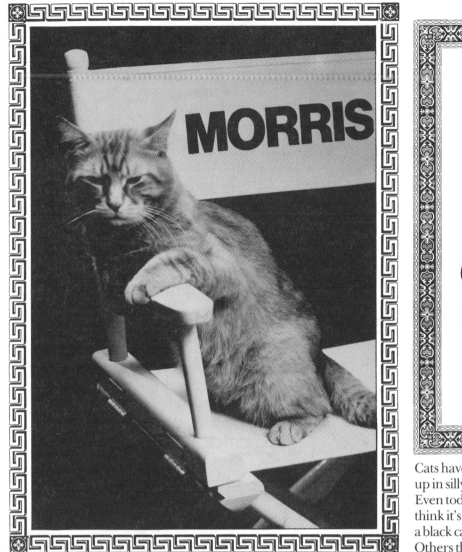

Cats have always been mixed up in silly superstitions. Even today, some people think it's unlucky to have a black cat cross their path. Others think it's lucky.

Who's the most finicky cat on television? Morris the 9-Lives cat, that's who.

Mamsell, who lives in Sunnybrook Hospital in Toronto, Canada, with some rabbits, birds and a few other animals, is a special companion to the elderly men in the hospital's extended care wing. Having a pet has been proven to be good for your health. Stroking and talking to your four-legged friend lowers your blood-pressure and some doctors feel that people live longer if they have pets to look after.

MIGHTY MITES

CAT TAIL ADVENTURES

Nick, Sophie and Mark Mite are three special kids with a big secret: they have discovered a way to shrink to any size they want and grow big again. When the Mites lose an important piece of a model bridge they are building, they shrink to find it and become involved in a strange cat and "mouse" hunt.

by Emily Hearn and Mark Thurman

WHERE'S THE CORD FOR THE PULLEYS?

HERE IT IS. I USED SOME OF IT FOR MY KITE.

WATCH THE PULLEY, NICK!

DARN IT! THE PULLEY'S ROLLED UNDER THE PIANO.

HERE, I'LL GET IT.

I CAN'T SQUEEZE MY ARM UNDER. THERE'S NO ROOM.

WE CAN SHRINK AND PUSH IT OUT.

THE MITES SHRINK

HEAVE!

ATCHOO!

WHO FORGOT TO DUST UNDER THE PIANO?

NOT ME.

NOT ME.

YIKES! MUGGINS WOKE UP!

RUN TO THE BACK OF THE PIANO. QUICK!

HOW SMART IS YOUR CAT?

**If you've ever been baffled by some of the
things your cat has done, this quiz is for you. If you
can answer yes to more than one or two of these
questions, you'll want to turn the page quickly.**

1. Does your cat watch television?

Yes ☐   No ☐

2. Have you ever caught your cat admiring itself
in the mirror?

Yes ☐   No ☐

3. Does your cat wash its paws under the faucet?

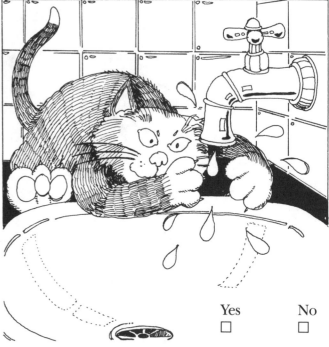

Yes ☐   No ☐

4. Can your cat open doors, cupboards or even
windows by itself?

Yes ☐   No ☐

5. Does your cat read newspapers or magazines?

Yes ☐ No ☐

8. Does your cat "talk" in its sleep?

Yes ☐ No ☐

6. Does your cat know when to wake you up in the morning?

7. Does your cat know that you've come home before anyone else in the house knows?

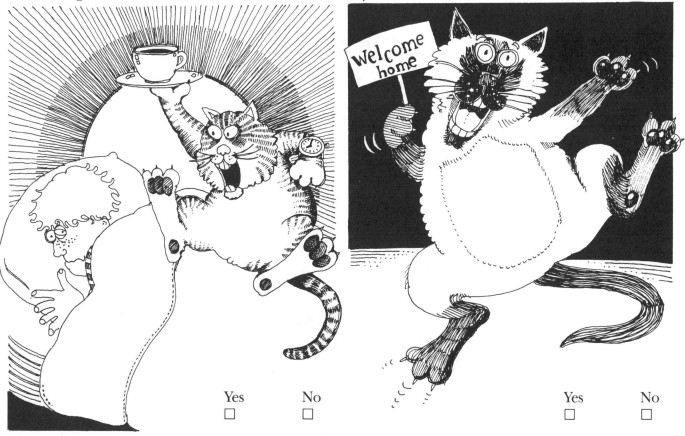

Yes ☐ No ☐

Yes ☐ No ☐

1. Does your cat watch television?

Some cat owners swear that their cat has its own favorite show and will even come running when it hears the theme music. But most cats don't really care what's on TV—they just like looking at the flickering movement of the picture. Why? Cats are attracted to any sort of fast movements—it's part of their hunting instinct. The flickering might remind your cat of small, scurrying animals.

But if you think that your cat is really intrigued by a particular television program—it may be that it becomes interested because it sees you watching the show.

2. Have you ever caught your cat admiring itself in the mirror?

For the same reason your cat may watch TV, it likes to look in the mirror—it's attracted to the movement it sees. And it seems it doesn't matter that the cat is the one making the movement.

3. Does your cat wash its paws under the faucet?

Even though most cats don't like getting wet, they will often be attracted by a dripping faucet. That's because of their fascination with any quick movement. In fact, some cats become so engrossed that they even try to catch the drips of water with their paws.

4. Can your cat open doors, or cupboards or even windows by itself?

When your cat tries to open doors or windows, it is simply showing its independence by coming and going as it pleases. Why are cats so independent? In the wild most cats are solitary animals compared with dogs, which hunt and live in packs and follow the commands of their pack leader. In fact, cats have been domesticated for only 3,500 years, unlike dogs, which have been man's best friend for close to 10,000 years.

5. Does your cat read newspapers or magazines?

If your cat jumps on your lap or shoulder while you're reading, it's probably more interested in the sound the pages are making than what's written on them. Cats are attracted to rustling and scratching noises. The noises sound like small animals running about in dry leaves and grass.

There might also be another reason why your cat jumps on your lap while you're reading: it wants to be the center of your attention, just like the book is.

7. Does your cat know that you've come home before anyone else in the house knows?

Cats can hear about six times better than you can. So it's not surprising that your cat can hear you coming before anyone else in your family can. In fact, some cats can distinguish their owner's footsteps from anybody else's—some can even recognize the sound of their owner's car engine.

6. Does your cat know when to wake you up in the morning?

Cats have an uncanny sense of time. Wild cats, for instance, will learn the movements of the animals around them and the best time to hunt them. In the same way, house cats easily learn the daily home routine, especially when to expect food. Some cats know their owners' schedule so well that they will even wake them a few minutes before the alarm is due to ring in the morning.

8. Does your cat "talk" in its sleep?

Your cat may not only talk, but its face may twitch and its legs "run" while it's asleep. Although scientists can't say for sure, they believe that many animals—including cats—dream at a certain stage of sleep. That stage is called rapid eye movement sleep, or "REM sleep" for short. If you look closely at your cat after it's been sleeping for a while, you can see its eyes flicker back and forth under its eyelids. That's REM sleep, which means there's a good chance that your cat is dreaming. And what do cats dream about? Some scientists think that a cat sorts out and stores away the events of its day while dreaming.

31

THE PATCHWORK CAT PUZZLE

Jumping jaguars! Here's a cat that we hope you never see. It has the body of a leopard, but beyond that almost everything else is wrong. There are eight things that make this cat unleopardlike. How many can you spot?

Answers on page 96

WHO'S WHO IN THE CAT WORLD

There are three families of wild cats—Panthera, Acinonyx and Felis. Thirty-seven species of cats belong to these family groups. Here are some of the most interesting.

Felis Family

**Caracal
(Felis caracal)**
35-50 lb. (16-23 kg)
The wonderfully agile

African caracal has such lighting-fast reflexes that it can grab birds out of the air.

Felis Family
Temmincks's Golden Cat (Felis temmincki)
14-24 lb. (6-11 kg)
This Southeast Asian cat with the striking golden coat is thought to live both in trees and on the ground. It hunts small rodents, and even deer.

Felis Family
Fishing Cat (Felis viverrina)
12-18 lb. (5.5-8 kg)
This Asian cat might not be a graceful walker, but it's a marvelous swimmer. No wonder—it has webbed feet.

Panthera Family

Leopard (Panthera pardus)
75-150 lb. (34-68 kg)
This cat—found throughout most of Africa and Asia—usually sports a spotted coat. But sometimes its coat can be completely black. Then this cat is called a black panther.

Felis Family

Bobcat
(Felis rufas)
15-35 lb. (7-16 kg)
These stocky cats can be found in most kinds of terrain from southern Canada to central Mexico. Male bobcats are unusual among cats because they help raise their young.

Felis Family
Serval
(Felis serval)
30-40 lb. (13.5-18 kg)
This African cat has big ears and long legs, the better to hear and then pounce upon small animals rustling in the grasslands where it lives.

Panthera Family
Clouded Leopard
(Panthera nebulosa)
30-45 lb. (13-20 kg)
This Asian cat has such long upper teeth that some people think it's related to the extinct saber-toothed tiger.

Felis Family

**Jungle Cat
(Felis chaus)**
16-30 lb. (7-13.5 kg)
Sometimes called the

"swamp cat," this cat of Asia
and Northeast Africa lurks
in marshes to ambush the
small animals it loves to eat.

CATS AT HOME

All house cats are members of the Felidae (or Felis) family of cats and share the scientific name *Felis catus*. In Canada there are over 30 breeds of domestic cat. Here's a look at some of the most interesting ones. Can you spot your breed of cat?

ABYSSINIAN

No one's sure if this rare cat is related to those painted on Egyptian tombs, but they're amazing look-alikes. They are very popular as pets because of their affectionate gentle personality, and because they are very alert and lively. The coat is soft but thick in shades of grey, brown and red.

AMERICAN (OR BRITISH) SHORTHAIR

Both the American and British shorthairs are medium to large cats, compact and well-muscled. They make good pets because of their intelligence and pleasant temperament. They come in a rainbow of solid colors, as well as the popular striped tabby.

BURMESE

This pretty little cat originally from Burma has a inquisitive face and very intelligent character. Some people think it has an almost "people-like" attitude. Its colors range from silvery and grey-blue to light and chocolate brown.

EGYPTIAN MAU

American and British breeders wanted to develop a cat that looked like the ones in ancient Egyptian art. They succeeded in the 1950's with this cat. Its body is similar to the Abyssinian. The patterns in its coat may be stripes or spots and the silky lustrous fur is silver, golden brown or dark grey.

EXOTIC SHORTHAIR
This robust cat looks like a Persian cat that's been to the barber shop. Its coat is very plush and dense but soft. These cats make great pets and come in many colors and patterns.

KORAT
This cat only comes in one colour—silvery blue. It's regarded as a good-luck cat in Thailand and was once so prized that no amount of silver could buy one. What makes it quite special is its almost heart-shaped face.

JAPANESE BOBTAIL
One look at this cat's rabbit-like tail and you can see how it got its name. It is a medium cat, well muscled but slender, with a soft silky coat. Each of these cats may be one solid color or a mixture of two or three.

RUSSIAN BLUE
These shy gentle cats were probably taken to Britain by Russian sailors hundreds of years ago. Its distinct feature is its bright blue double coat, which is very soft and shiny. All Russian Blues have green eyes.

MANX
No, this cat hasn't had a door slammed on its tail—it never had one! Its compact body is almost bear-like. The Manx cat is an intelligent affectionate cat. It is short-haired and comes in a broad spectrum of colors and patterns.

SCOTTISH FOLD

This cat is easy to recognize because of its sad expression and its floppy ears which refuse to stand up. It is a sturdy cat and can come in a wide variety of colors and patterns.

SIAMESE

Lithe, elegant, intelligent and loyal are some descriptions of the popular Siamese. These are very dainty cats with affectionate talkative natures. All Siamese have cream to light-brown bodies, but the markings (called points) on their ears, paws and face can range from pinkish to bluish to dark brown.

OCICAT

The Ocicat is quite large and looks athletic and graceful. It once reminded its American breeder of an ocelot—and that's how it got its name. It comes in several colors, but all have the spotted coat pattern.

TONKINESE

What do you get when you cross a Siamese with a Burmese cat? A rare breed called the Tonkinese. It is a medium-sized, elegant cat with an out-going and affectionate nature. You can find examples of this breed in many different colors.

BALINESE

This breed is known as the Javanese in the United States. It is a very dainty looking cat but is lithe and strong as well. It resembles the Siamese, except for its long-haired coat. The Balinese are born acrobats and make very affectionate pets. Like the Siamese, its points or markings come in a range of shades.

CHARTREUX
Carthusian monks brought this cat to France from South Africa centuries ago. It is a large, robust and nicely proportioned cat, which is generally only grey-blue with silvery highlights.

BIRMAN
This cat (also known as the Sacred Cat of Burma) is thought to be a direct descendant of the sacred cats that once guarded the temples in that country. Its body is large and low on its legs. Its coloring is similar to that of the Siamese but it looks like it's wearing white socks.

CORNISH REX
The coat of this cat is wavy and because it does not have heavy outer hairs, it feels warm and velvety. This breed is intelligent, outgoing and affectionate. The Devon Rex is very similar in the texture of its coat but the shape of its head, which is almost elf-like, makes it unique. Both breeds come in many colors and patterns and neither one sheds its fur.

CYMRIC
Like its cousin the Manx, this cat has no tail. It, too, is of medium build and bear-like. But the Cymric has semi-long hair, unlike the Manx cat's short hair. This long-haired cousin is affectionate, too, and comes in many colors.

PERSIAN
The face of a Persian cat is very distinctive—rounded, open and sweet-looking. Its body is short with thick heavy bones although that is difficult to see because of its long flowing coat. Persians are famous for their gentle temperament, and come in a wide variety of colors and patterns.

HIMALAYAN

This cat resembles a Persian, but has markings similar to a Siamese. Its coat is long and fine. Deep blue eyes are one of its most striking features. As well as being a very beautiful cat, it is gentle and entertaining and makes a good pet.

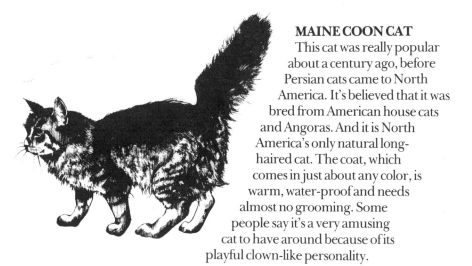

MAINE COON CAT

This cat was really popular about a century ago, before Persian cats came to North America. It's believed that it was bred from American house cats and Angoras. And it is North America's only natural long-haired cat. The coat, which comes in just about any color, is warm, water-proof and needs almost no grooming. Some people say it's a very amusing cat to have around because of its playful clown-like personality.

TURKISH ANGORA

Don't mistake this pretty cat for a Persian. It not only has a smaller head, but also has a longer body and tail than the Persian breed. And it's not from Persia, but from the Turkish city of Ankara. These cats are very flexible and have semi-long hair in a wide variety of colors and patterns.

RAGDOLL

Hold one of these unique cats in your arms and you'd swear you were holding a limp ragdoll. But their bodies are firm and muscular and their coat is thick, soft and silky. Some of these cats may be one solid color, or a mixture of two colors, some may have different-colored feet, or have points like a Siamese. Most come in shades of grey or brown.

FAMILY TREE

40 MILLION YEARS AGO
MIACIS

PRESENT
DOGS

PRESENT
HYAENAS

EXTINCT
20 MILLION YEARS AGO
NIMRAVIES
(Cat-like carnivores)

SABERTOOTHS
LAST SPECIES
EXTINCT 10,000
YEARS AGO

**20 MILLION
YEARS AGO
FAMILY OF
FELIDS**

PRESENT
RACCOONS

PRESENT
**"ACINONYX" CAT
CHEETAH**

PRESENT
**"PANTHERA" CATS
BIG CATS**

PRESENT
**FELIS CATS
SMALL CATS**

CAT WAYS

On the following pages, you'll have a chance
to see how wild cats behave. That will help explain
why your pet cat does the things it does...

Washing Up

This African wild cat is careful about washing after meals because leftover blood on its face or paws would attract flies and, possibly, enemies. To wash the top of its head, this cat —like all others—will moisten its favorite front paw and use it as a face cloth. Then it does the same on the opposite side with the other paw. Next, it will lick each shoulder and front leg in turn, then it will clean its sides and back legs. It usually saves its tail for the last. Does your cat follow the same order when it washes itself?

Cooling Down

This tiger has just woken up from a deep sleep in the sun and is feeling hot. There's no stream nearby for a quick dip so it will do the next best thing to cool down. It will—like all other cats—groom itself by wetting its fur with its tongue. As the saliva evaporates, it cools down the entire body. So if you see your cat washing up after playing, running or climbing, chances are it's trying to cool down.

Being a Friend

This leopard mother spends a lot of time licking her babies. She's doing more than cleaning them: she's showing them affection. When adult cats (wild and domestic) groom each other, usually after meals and before settling down to sleep, it's a sign of friendliness. So as you pat your cat you are, in a way, grooming it too and saying, "I'm your friend."

Dream Time

If you could listen to these lions, you might hear them muttering and purring. That and the twitching of their ears and tails would tell you that they've probably finished a good meal, are sleeping deeply and possibly dreaming, too. They'll know you are there, however, as their hearing, even while asleep, is very acute. Lions, like all cats, take many cat naps as quick pick-me-ups.

Odd Snoozes

It's not unusual for a sleepy lion to stretch out along a narrow tree branch and snooze with its head and legs dangling down. This may look uncomfortable to you, but the lion finds it quite cozy. Your cat may have equally unusual sleeping spots and positions. Though it may curl up in a soft armchair, it can just as easily perch on a concrete ledge and sleep. However, no matter where they sleep, all cats like to stay warm. That's why your cat will stretch out in a sunny spot or in front of the fire, but will roll up into a tight ball in a cool or drafty spot.

45

Getting Around

Look at these caracal tracks. They are different from those made by most four-footed animals: you could connect them with a straight line. That's because the caracal, like all other cats, is one of the few animals (along with the giraffe and camel) that can walk or run by moving front and back legs on one side and then front and back legs on the other. No wonder your cat can walk along the head-board of your bed and not fall off.

Whiz

This African cheetah—the fastest animal on earth—is moving at 100 km/h (62 mph). Like all cats, however, it is a sprinter, not a long-distance runner. Cats have small chests and lungs, so after a spurt of speed—which is all they need to leap on their dinner—they must rest. That's why your house cat won't try to out-run a dog over a long distance. It would rather escape by climbing up a tree or jumping onto a fence.

Being able to take long and high jumps—five times or more their own height—is something all cats are built for, as they have to pounce on their prey to catch it. It's not surprising, therefore, that your cat can leap to the top of the refrigerator with ease.

Watch your cat the next time it jumps down from the refrigerator. Does it shake its paws or lick its paw pads? If so, that means it had a hard—not gentle—landing.

46

Climbing

These African leopards are getting up a tree in two very catlike ways. One is hitching its way up by using its strong claws as hooks, while the other is going up the easy way: in a single leap. These cats will lurk in branches until a meal comes by and then they will drop down.

Going up a tree is something a house cat generally does with ease too, but coming down is quite a different matter and takes a bit of practice. That's because your cat cannot turn its paws sideways to get a good grip. Although it will be awkward and look a bit strange, a cat will come down head first. It's more likely to climb down part of the way and then jump. And contrary to what people think, a cat rarely gets stuck up a tree. If you wait long enough, the cat will usually come down safely on its own.

The South American margay, on the other hand, is one of the few cats that can run down a tree head-first. Unlike your cat, the margay has ankle and foot joints that swivel so it can turn its paws around for a good grip.

Marking a Scent

This mother cheetah has returned to her cubs. They greet each other by touching cheeks and rubbing the whole side of their bodies against one another. They are doing more than saying hello—they are marking each other as friendly territory.

Your house cat does the same. All cats have scent glands on each side of their forehead and on their lips, chin and tail. When your cat winds itself around your legs, it's marking you with scent from these glands. Even two friendly cats will mark each other in this way.

Establishing Territory

This Canada lynx occupies a territory and will defend it against intruders. Your cat—even though it probably doesn't need to hunt for food—has a territory too. In a crowded city, your cat's "turf" may be no bigger than a back garden or an apartment, while in the country it may be 10 times as large. Like its wild cousins, your cat has favorite resting spots within its territory. That may be one reason why your cat always sleeps in the same armchair—even if you're trying to sit there, too.

Kneading for Affection

Sometimes your cat may pause from winding around your legs to knead its paws on the floor, almost as if it were playing an imaginary piano. When it does this, it's following an old instinct. Young cats (wild and domestic) press their paws against their mother's teat to make the milk flow. When your cat presses its paws against furniture or even your lap, it's feeling happy. But it's not looking for milk—it's looking for affection.

THE HUNT

Cats, like the cougar you see here, are very good at teaching their young. So, a hunt can be more than just a way to get a meal. It is also an important survival lesson for the young.

It's a warm August night and a full moon is rising over the Rocky Mountains. In the tall meadow grass a female cougar swiftly lowers her head and drops into a crouch. She has just caught the scent of a deer. Almost invisible in the moonlight, she creeps noiselessly forward on fur-padded feet. At last the cat

sees what her nose has already told her is there: a lone deer is grazing on the sweet grass.

The deer is nervous because the rest of the herd has moved on, but can't resist such a fine feast. Suddenly he looks up. The cougar freezes and only when the deer begins eating again does she continue to creep forward. Her belly is to the ground and her eyes never once leave the prey. All that betrays her excitement is a slight swish of her tail. Pausing, she wiggles her hips, winding up for her one chance of bringing down the unsuspecting deer.

Suddenly, the cougar springs. The deer staggers and frantically tries to throw the terrifying weight off its shoulders. But it's no use. With lightning speed the cougar's strong teeth sink into her prey's neck, and it's all over.

The cougar is very hungry, but before eating she turns her head and makes a soft noise. The grass behind her rustles, and out of a hiding place bounds a very hungry cub, too young to hunt, but just old enough to watch how his mother does it. This is only the second night he's been allowed to watch. Last night he made so much noise he scared everything away—no wonder they're both so hungry.

Mother and cub settle down to a well-earned meal, feeding until they can eat no more. Then, copying his mother, the cub helps to hide the leftovers under a pile of dirt, twigs and leaves. That takes care of tomorrow's dinner. Now it's time to pad home to their snug den and sleep away what's left of the night.

The cub is learning fast. When he was born a year ago he was a spotted bundle of fluff, no bigger than a six-week-old domestic kitten. Days were spent nursing and cuddling up to his mother's soft fur until in just a few weeks he was romping outside the den under his mother's watchful eye. Even at that early age, although he didn't know it, the cub was playing games that would help develop hunting skills. He never tired of these games, especially jumping on his mother's gently waving tail. And she didn't mind at all. It was all part of raising a young cougar.

At three months of age, still too young to go hunting with his mother, the cub waited patiently in the den for her return. He knew she'd be bringing back several chunks of meat. To encourage him to pounce on his meat, the mother cougar would bat it about with her paws before letting him eat.

Every day the cub grew stronger and larger. It wasn't long before his mother started taking her cub to the place where she had caught her prey. And at last the moment arrived when he was allowed to watch his mother in action.

Night after night over the next year he would go out with his mother, carefully watching the way she stalked and paused, when she jumped and how. Finally, it was time for him to try catching his own food. His first attempts were bound to fail—it takes skill to know how far and how fast to leap.

And even when he did manage to land on a deer's shoulders, at first he fell off until he learned to concentrate and balance well enough to hang on.

His mother will stay by him until he's two years old, teaching him patiently, by example, how to correct his mistakes. Then it will be time for her to move on, find a mate and have more cubs, which she'll raise in just the same way.

Hunting at Home

Like its wild cousin, the cougar, your house cat has a strong instinct to hunt. First it will stalk its prey, then pounce, reaching out with its front paws to pin down its victim. Next, instinct tells your cat to bite at the narrow neck area.

Even though instinct tells all cats where to bite their prey, they have to practice finding the special spot in the neck where they can sink in their teeth and give the killing bite. Some cats, especially those raised by nonhunting mothers, never learn how to give the killing bite. Your cat may be one of these. If you have ever seen your cat pounce on live prey, only to let it go and pounce on it again, it isn't playing a cruel game. Your cat may not have been taught to kill, even though it knows how to hunt.

Usually a cat, wild or domestic, gobbles up its prey after catching it. But sometimes the kill is large enough to last a couple of days. When that happens, the cat may hide the leftovers in a secluded spot. A mother cat will either lead her young to that spot or will take the food home. In fact, your house cat may even bring home a mouse or other prey that is has hunted. If it does, it's following the ways of its wild cousins.

TIGERS ARE TERRIFIC!

Stunning markings, graceful agility and
a muscular body make the tiger one of the most
splendid of all cats.

Silent Prowler

Everything about the tiger—from its superb eyesight and hearing to its tail—seems to have been designed especially for hunting. As dusk falls, the tiger sets out on its silent prowl through the jungle. Once it spies its prey, it stalks it for hours, if necessary, hiding behind every available piece of cover until it's close enough to pounce—then it launches into the air, its fangs bared and claws ready to strike. The impact of a tiger on an animal is so tremendous that even a wild bull, four times as heavy as the tiger, can't withstand the impact.

Big Appetite

A tiger can eat as much meat in one day as you would eat in a month. If it can't hide its kill, or easily guard it from scavengers, it'll gulp down the equivalent of ten roasts of beef all at once. Tigers in captivity are fed 6 kg (13 lb.) a day which is probably closer to what they would usually eat in the wild on an average day.

Private Property— Keep Out

Because a tiger needs so much meat, its hunting territory has to be large. To make sure that other tigers don't trespass, a tiger will leave scent markings. The scent they spray, just like domestic cats, is urine.

Calling Cards

When other tigers come across a marked territory, they'll spray their own scents around its boundary. This tells the "owner" who's in the neighborhood. If one of the visiting tigers is female, she might even be invited in.

One of a Kind

A tiger's pattern of stripes is as individual as your fingerprints—no two are alike. One sure way to tell one tiger from another is to look at the black and white markings above the eyes—each tiger has a different patch.

Cool Cats

Can you imagine your cat wanting to go for a swim? Most cats hate getting wet, but a tiger loves to play in water to cool off and clear parasites out of its fur. Also the water is a fine place to find tasty fish and turtles. During a drought, a tiger will travel far to find water and will even dig for it in dry river beds.

No Room for Tigers

At one time seven distinct races of tiger roamed the entire Asian continent. Today, one of these races—the Balinese—is extinct. In fact, there are only between 5,000 and 7,000 tigers in all left in the wild. What happened? As people needed more land for farming, they used up the tiger's hunting grounds, so there are fewer places for tigers to live. Also many tigers are killed for their skins, or to protect villages and livestock. Fortunately, the countries where tigers still exist are beginning to protect them and organizations such as the World Wildlife Fund help by raising money to maintain reserves where tigers can live in safety.

CAMOUFLAGE

If you were the deer in this picture you might be able to smell at least one tiger, but you wouldn't be able to see it. That's partly because the tiger's black stripes blend perfectly with the strong shadows found in both the green jungles and dry, grassy areas where it lives. But it's also likely that, as a deer, you'd see green and orange as the same color. To you, the big cat would be just another stripy pattern—until it leaps!

CAT CHAT

Cats communicate by sound and action. And cat "street talk" isn't much different from cat "jungle talk". Experts say that cats make 16 different sounds.

Scientists know that cats purr when they are happy, or getting a lot of attention. But they also purr as a greeting or a request for food or attention. For a long time scientists weren't really sure how cats purred. One theory was that the purring noise was caused by blood rushing through a large blood vessel in the cat's chest. They now know however, that purring results when a cat vibrates the muscles of its throat and diaphragm.

CAT CHAT

A cat's first signal to "beware" is standing very still, staring. Next its tail swishes and its fur stands on end. Sensible intruders don't receive the final warning—a snarl and a show of sharp teeth—they're long gone.

MEOW

Have you ever seen a cat lift and twitch its whiskers and widen its pupils? If so, you know the cat is concentrating on something or someone of interest.

A loud meow generally means, "Listen to me, I want something".

The high pitched howl you sometimes hear is the sound of fighting or mating behavior. This is known as a caterwaul.

A hiss says, "I'm annoyed, stay away."

Purrr...

Ever wonder why some cats and dogs don't get along? It might be because they talk different languages. To a cat a swishing tail means, "Go away," but it means just the opposite to a dog.

MEOW

58

This cat is very happy and secure. You can tell because of its "belly-up" position. Some wild cats lie on their backs too, especially after a satisfactory meal.

growl

This cat's scratches say, "Keep away." Most cats stake out their property by scratching, or they leave their scent by urinating or rubbing against things.

My territory

OOW EEOW

Any cat owner knows that dogs aren't the only pets that growl. While a cat may not growl as loudly or as often, when it does, its "ready to attack" message comes through loud and clear.

If you looked only at a cat's ears and tail, you'd know a lot about how it feels. If its ears are bent forward, the cat is curious; held back to the sides, it is nervous. Ears flattened back mean anger.

Mother cats purr to calm their young. For the first two weeks of life, before their sense of hearing has developed, kittens don't hear these lullabies at all, but they do feel the vibrations.

rrrrrrrr

GRRREAT CATS

Many wild cats today need help from people to survive. Here are three true stories about great cats and people who care for them.

STORY #1: LOOKING AFTER LIONS

As a young girl, Barbara Chupa fed cows, horses, dogs and cats on a friend's farm. Now she helps care for animals at the Metropolitan Toronto Zoo in Canada. Here's her story of looking after the large lions in the zoo.

I've always loved animals and it's no different today, except for one thing: now I look after lions named Natasha, Nosey, Brenda, Virginia, Jewel and Butch. The Metro Toronto Zoo has been their home for the past 12 years. During that time they've got to know me very well. They even know I'm nearby before they see me because they recognize the familiar jingle-jangle of my keys that open up the lion house. They prick up their ears expectantly and often one of the female lions will make a soft moaning sound in her throat. Soon the others follow suit, until the lion house is filled with sounds of the lion chorus.

This sound is often the loudest when the lions know it's time for me to serve them their one meal of the day. They eat in their own pens inside the lion house. That's because the lions are very possessive about their food, but, more important, each lion gets an individual dinner prepared especially for it with just the right mix of nutrients. Butch is the biggest eater of all, gobbling up 5 kg (11 lb.) of feline diet (a mixture of ground meat and vitamins) a day, while the females each eat about 3 kg (6½ lb.) of food a day. It takes the lions about a minute to eat their meal. That's the same as you gulping down between 25 and 40 hamburgers in just 60 seconds!

The lions wash down their meal with plenty of fresh drinking water and twice a week they gnaw big bones to help clean their teeth.

Next to eating, the lions' favorite activity is snoozing. In spring and summer months, they sleep outdoors in their enclosed compound, preferably in a nice sunny spot. I keep a very close eye on the lions while they eat, snooze and play. I'm on the alert for any signs of distress or illness. If I spot any problem, I immediately report it to one of the zoo veterinarians.

I love the lions, but above all I respect them. After all, you can't forget that they are wild animals.

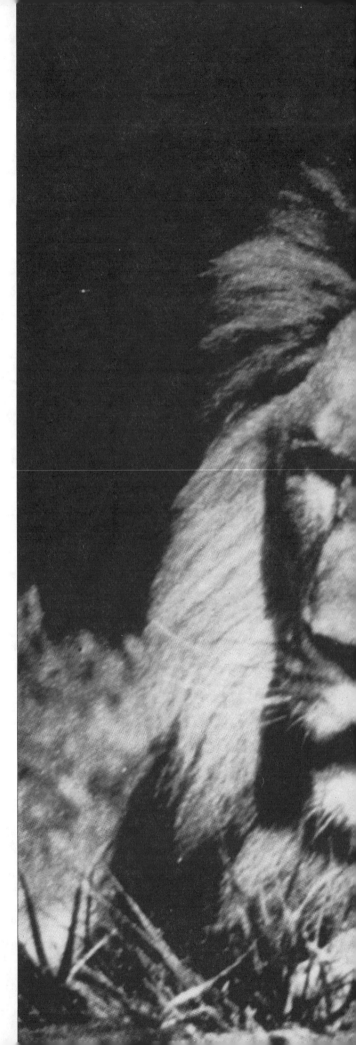

STORY #2: SAVING THE TIGERS

"You never forget your first sight of a wild tiger."

Everyone who has seen tigers in the wild agrees. Somehow they look different from those you see in a zoo. They walk with a confident stride, their muscles rippling and bulging, and their striped orange and black fur gleams like satin. When tigers are in their own environment they look free.

Thousands of tigers once roamed Asia. Although they were hunted for sport, early hunters used bows and arrows, and the odds were in favor of the tigers. But by the 17th century guns were invented, and real trouble for tigers began. People could shoot them without getting too close, and they did—by the thousands. Then people began poisoning tigers because the tiger skins were more valuable if they were free of bullet holes.

If all this wasn't bad enough, the jungles where tigers lived began to be destroyed by people who needed the space, too. Trees were logged out and forests were burned to clear land for farms. Then the wars in Korea and Vietnam further destroyed the rich rain forests that gave tigers and other animals the food and shelter they needed to survive.

WANTED

ALIVE

for its beauty, grace, and contribution to the living world.
Fifty years ago there were 100,000 tigers.
Now there are barely 5,000.
The tiger is doomed unless we act now.

Support Operation Tiger

the World Wildlife Fund's International Campaign to save
the tiger and its forest home.

REWARD

satisfaction at having helped to save
a species threatened with extinction.

In 1930 there were 100,000 tigers in Asia. Fifty years later there were only 5,000! It was only then—and almost too late—people realized that the tiger might disappear altogether.

It was just a few people who started the fight to save the tiger from extinction. But soon they were joined by thousands around the world. Saving the tiger meant buying land for reserves where tigers could live, and for this nearly $2 million had to be raised. Kids everywhere also pitched in, buying T-shirts, collecting money and even campaigning against tiger-skin coats. Children in Holland alone raised nearly $600,000.

With so many people helping, the money was raised in just 18 months and work of moving tigers into the reserved areas where they could be protected began. With the success of the first reserves in India, other countries where tigers were endangered moved to protect them.

Ten years ago there seemed little hope of saving tigers from total extinction. Today, in many countries the tiger population is on the increase. So this is a story with a happy ending after all.

Footnote: For more information on how kids can help wildlife, contact the World Wildlife Fund office at 60 St. Clair Ave. E., Toronto, Ontario, M4T 1N5.

STORY #3: LOOKING OUT FOR LYNXES

Lynxes in Sweden (they are called *lodjur* there) may be luckier than most. That's because Stefan Jonsson, one of the best friends lynxes have, lives there, too. There are few of these short-tailed, medium-sized wild cats left, and Stefan is trying to protect them. Over the years he has come to know them very well. He shares here some of his love for these beautiful animals.

As part of my work helping lynxes, I sometimes raise orphaned or injured cats from the wild, and this has been a wonderful way to study them. I've learned that a young hand-reared lynx is quite tame and very lovable. I know how exciting it is to see a lynx kitten's eyes open for the first time on its tenth day of life. But for me, the best way to see a lynx is in the wild.

When you see a lynx in its own environment you can see why people once thought these cats could look right through wooden walls. A lynx's big bright eyes seem unbelievably keen when they shine at you through a dense pine forest.

I've seen a number of families in the wild, and I am always thrilled by them. A mother lynx is so pro-

tective. For example, she always lets her kittens eat first. And when she leaves them in March to find a mate, she kills one or two roe-deer for them to feed on while she's gone.

Then, when she returns in about ten days, she begins their hunting lessons very seriously. They must learn to be on their own by the time food is plentiful in summer.

Seeing a very young kitten in the wild is a very special
event for me, and it gives me new encouragement
to help these beautiful animals. I know that it is
difficult for people and wild animals to live together
—people need the land and so do the animals. But
it's important we all try to find a way.

BASIC BREEDING

People began to breed cats seriously in the 19th century to get showy cats of special colors, coats and body shapes. Even today, new breeds of cats are being developed. Here's a look at some interesting breeding facts that people have discovered through the years.

A pedigreed cat has a family tree of five generations. Such a cat—one with similar-looking great-great-great-grandparents—is usually officially registered and recognized by a cat association.

A female cat can have as many as 100 kittens in her lifetime.

Normal kittens are born with blue eyes. If the color changes (to green, copper, etc.), the change begins at about three weeks of age.

A Siamese kitten is born almost white. Its face, paws and tail gradually darken, as its body becomes a slightly richer colour.

White cats with blue eyes are usually deaf. Sometimes (although very rarely) white cats with orange eyes are deaf, too. Odd-eyed white cats (cats with one blue and one orange eye) can usually hear very well. But sometimes the ear closer to the blue eye is deaf.

If a cat with a normal length tail mates with a tailless Manx (see page 38), the kittens will probably be tailless too.

If two black cats mate, you might thing that black kittens would be the result. But some turn out to be tabby-patterned. That's because what a kitten looks like depends on its genes (a "blueprint" of instructions in every living thing). A kitten's genes are inherited from its parents, whose genes were passed along from their parents, and so on. So if two black cats produce a tabby, one of their grandparents was probably a tabby, too. It's the same as you inheriting your grandfather's blue eyes when everyone else in your family has brown eyes.

Mate a Siamese with a Burmese and you'll get a Tonkinese cat—a breed of cat all itself (see page 39). But mate two Tonkinese cats and you'll probably not only get Tonkinese kittens, but Siamese and Burmese, too.

A cat with a blaze of white on its face and nose will usually pass this patch on to its kittens.

If a long-haired cat mates with a short-haired one, chances are most of their kittens will have short hair. But these kittens may carry genes for long hair and so later on become parents of kittens with long hair.

CAT LOG

Here's a chart for jotting down facts about your pet cat. If you run out of room, you can make your own charts in a small notebook and even include photographs or drawings of your cat.

name of cat

breed

age

sex

length

(_____ weeks)
(_____ weeks)
(_____ weeks)
(_____ weeks)
(_____ weeks)
(_____ weeks)

height

(_____ weeks)
(_____ weeks)
(_____ weeks)
(_____ weeks)
(_____ weeks)
(_____ weeks)

color(s) of cat

color of eyes

color of nose

length of whiskers

paw prints

Why I love my cat

name and number of vet _____

annual check-up date _____ shots _____

favorite food(s) _____

favorite sleeping spot _____

most unusual sleeping position _____

favorite game _____

favorite toy _____

The most interesting thing I've ever seen my cat do _____

The silliest thing I've ever seen my cat do _____

Things that make my cat purr _____

distinguishing marks or features _____

THE NAMING OF CATS

**"The naming of cats is a difficult matter.
It isn't just one of your holiday games...
I will tell you a cat needs a name that's particular.
A name that's peculiar and more dignified,
Else how can he keep up his tail perpendicular
Or spread out his whiskers, or cherish his pride?"**
                                        T.S. Eliot.

Here's our collection of "particular and peculiar
names"—all real. Is your cat's name mentioned?

Adam
Alberta Gold
Amanda Rose
Amy
Antalya Anatolia
Arthur

Blackwell Jogram
Bamboo Betula
Banana Split
Barrose Honeybear
Beach Girl
Be-Jer
Belcanto Zigeunerbaron
Bilbo's Petrushka
Billy Joe
Black Magic
Blue Bell
Blue Jeans
Bonaventura
Bonavia Flute
Bonnie Boy
Bootsie
Bourneside Cream Puff
Bruton Angelo
Bubbles

Carla
Calypso
Carpan
Carstep's Joliesse
Cendrillon
Chester
Chiang
Chicquot Milady
Chiuming Claudius
Cinnamon
Clouseau
Colombo
Contented Penny
Culverden Edward

Dancing Diana
Dandy
Deebank Magnus
Deverest
De Vincent Beatrice
Dickens
Dixiecrest Dreamtime
Dusty

Echo
Elan Ali Baba

Felix
Floralie Teddy Bear
Fluffy
Foss
Frances

Garfield
Gay
George
Giroflee
Gitan
Golden Charmer
Gossip
Gowlaven Orpheus
Gray-Ivy Keepsake

Hamlet
Harrison
Heidi
Henderson
Hi-Fi's Schwartz
Hihoe Persuasio
Hodge

Jasper
Jazreel Murrey
Jeoffrey
Jerba's Honey

Kala Yasmeen
Kalinka
Kallibunker
Kato
Kastamonou Yaladi
Katrina
Kitty
Killer
Kim
Kirelee
Kristi

Laicha's Sissi
Lecreme Arcturus
Louis
Lucky Star
Lucy's Kitten

Mabelle
Maha Rajah
Maggie Muffins
Mafeking King-Tut
Maid
Maple Leaf Montego
Mansel Gronski
Marlu Dandrift
Mary Lou Azale
Mateus
Maybeline
Meisha Caramel
Merlika
Merlin
Michael Patrick
Mickey
Midnight
Milord O'Mendip
Minnie
Miss Mibbs
Morris
Mystral Milovlee

Narcisse
Natasha
Nevern Una

Ora Song
Owen's Tango

Pdee's Trumpet
Peachy Parody
Peela Genevieve
Peerless Firecrest
Persephone
Pitapet Sequins

Plantaganet Vetta
Poopsie
Pracha Shawnee

Redmie Josephine
Red Red Robin
Ronaldkirk Admiral
Rutherford
Rosine
Rose Anah Danah

Saeng Dara's Swinger
Saphir
Scooter
Scibbles
Selima
Stanley
Shaughnessy
Slippers
Smithway Juliet
Snow Jewel
Solitaire Amethyst
Sonata Sovranino
Sue Mister-Su
Sugar Daddy of Dunesk
Sunan
Sweet Fire
Sylvester

Taisum Leo
Thaiquan Typhoo
Theodore
Tiffanee
Tiger
Tom
Torrington Sunnysides
Tuffy
Tusket

Van Fethiye
Vel-Ven-Voo Doo
Vida Tamar

Waldo
Walter
Wilkie
Williaminna
Wilmar Whimsy

Zenith Estella
Zephyr Dionysus
Zig Zag
Zimalus Chocolate Fudge

KITTENS

How do you come up with a name that suits your new kitten? You can't be sure whether it will grow up to be an aristocat or an average cat-about-the house, but you can tell something about its character by observing it. And what you learn may give you an idea for a name. Why not practice kitten naming by seeing what names you can come up with for the kittens on the next few pages.

MY NEW KITTENS

Tips on kitten care from a diary by Rachael Harry, 12

I knew as soon as I saw those little black kittens exactly what their names should be: Mercedes, Blue and Beethoven. I liked Mercedes the best. Not only was she the fluffiest, she was the most mischievous.

My family was very careful to leave the kittens and their mother alone as much as possible when the kittens were newborns. But Rebecca, their mom, hardly ever left them. She always seemed to be feeding them and licking them clean. And by keeping the kittens close to her at all times she was making sure that their temperature was constant so they wouldn't get sick.

When the kittens were born their upper and lower eyelids were stuck together, and it wasn't until they were about ten days old that they could see at all. How helpless they were. I'm glad they had such an excellent mother.

When they were about ten days old our kittens started crawling, pulling themselves along in short wobbly steps. It was really cute to watch. But while I was looking at them I also noticed that they waggled their heads back and forth as if searching for their mother's nipple. From time to time they also kneaded their mother's stomach with their paws while they fed. Perhaps that's why some adult cats—even Rebecca—make kneading motions when they sit on your lap. I think maybe they remember their mothers and want some food.

I found out that when they are very young, kittens can't hear very well, either. Maybe that's a good thing, because ours squeaked so loudly and so often. It didn't take me long to realize that the kittens did this to attract their mother's attention.

10-28 Days

I love Mercedes so much. Now that she has learned to walk without toppling over she has found coffee cups very interesting. Even when they are full. What a mess! Now our kittens' teeth have started to appear. These new teeth don't seem to make the kittens more fierce, but I guess they are important because soon the kittens will take food other than milk.

35-50 Days

Rebecca has started to wean her kittens. The first time I put milk in a saucer for her kittens they thought it was a paddling pool, but a week or so later they were lapping it up.

Rebecca has taught her kittens how to use the kitty litter. That's why I like cats—they're so clean and independent.

Because we already have Rebecca, my family decided that Mercedes and her brothers should go to new homes. I was sad but proud to know that their new owners would have such nice kittens. I hoped I would be able to see them as they grew into cats.

28-35 Days

It is hilarious to see the kittens jump on each other. They pounce, miss and collapse on the floor in furry balls of fluff. One of their favorite tricks now is to tease poor old Rebecca. They lie and hide and wait and attack her tail as if they are huge ferocious tigers hunting prey.

CHOOSING A CAT

A cat makes a wonderful pet, provided you are prepared to spend enough time and energy to care for it properly. Here are some pointers.

DO

Pick a cat that's right for your family. Would you be happier with a quiet (Persian) or a talkative (Siamese) cat? Does a hardy, affectionate British or American shorthair appeal to you more than an active, inquisitive cat like a Rex? Would you prefer a beautiful and glamorous cat with long hair (that needs daily brushing), or a short-haired variety that requires less grooming?

Pick an alert, calm and friendly cat. A shy cat may make a very timid pet, while one that bites and claws may not make friends with your other friends.

DON'T

Pick the runt of the litter. It may look cute, but it might have health problems later because of its size.

DON'T

Bring a new pet home at Christmas or at any other festive occasion. The noise and excitement might make it hard for the cat to settle into its new home.

DO

Get a kitten when it's about 6 to 8 weeks old, which is when specialists feel is the best time for a kitten to get used to a new home. Most kittens can begin to eat solid food by the time they are 4 weeks old and can be weaned from their mother as early as 6 weeks.

FEEDING... AND CARING

Keeping your cat happy and healthy is a big responsibility. Here are some tips to help.

Check with your vet on what is best to feed your cat. Most recommend a varied diet with no one food eaten exclusively. A varied diet is not only nutritious, but will help prevent your cat from becoming a finicky eater.

When feeding your cat commercial cat food, look for brands that are low in ash (magnesium). Try to alternate among canned, moist, semi-moist and dry so your cat gets lots of flavors and textures.

Try not to serve fresh or canned food straight from the refrigerator. Food that's cold may upset some cats' stomachs. Let the food warm to room temperature first.

Cats sometimes eat grass. This is good for them generally and may help any hair they swallow while grooming to pass through their system. If your cat is indoors most of the time, you might consider growing grass, oats, wheat or alfalfa sprouts in a pot for your cat to nibble. Check with your vet first.

Cats are possessive about their food, so if you have more than one cat, offer each its own feeding bowl.

Always wash a cat's dishes separately from the family dishes.

Help keep your cat's teeth clean by offering it chewy food (liked cooked chicken gizzards) or dry food (with plenty of water on the side) to munch occasionally. Brushing your cat's teeth is also a great way to help keep the teeth and gums healthy. Speak to your vet about how to do this—never use people toothpaste.

Don't encourage your cat to overeat by leaving food out in its dish once meals are finished. Give your cat about 10 minutes or so to eat, then remove its dish. The only exception to this is leaving out a bowl of dry or semi-moist food for your cat if you are going to be away for several hours and will not be able to feed it at its regular mealtime. Always leave plenty of fresh water for your cat to wash its dry food down. However, if you are going to be away for a long period of time, it's best to make arrangements with a friend or relative to feed your cat.

Don't force your adult cat to drink milk—it may cause diarrhea.

Kittens should eat three to four small meals a day, while most adult cats need just one big meal—or perhaps two small ones—a day.

And older cats (those over 10 years old) find it easier to digest several small meals—instead of one big one—a day.

82

Make your house safe for your cat. Cover fish tanks, put a screen over open fireplaces, keep dryer, washing machine and oven doors closed. And (especially if you and your cat live in a highrise building) have an adult make sure that your pet cannot accidentally slip out of any windows or under balcony railings.

Give your cat its own bed in a quiet corner away from drafts. Many prefer a cardboard box or wicker basket that's padded with an old, but soft, towel or blanket. Add a hot water bottle wrapped in a blanket for a kitten on cold nights.

Keep your cat's litter tray on top of newspapers in a quiet corner. Empty, clean and disinfect the tray regularly.

Cats need to clean and sharpen their claws regularly on rough surfaces. If your cat cannot get outside to scratch its claws on a tree it might start using the furniture to sharpen its claws. The best thing to do is provide it with a scratching post. You can buy a scratching post at a pet store or make your own by covering a board or a pole with strong fabric—carpet or burlap.

If your cat will not use a scratching post and is destructive in the house with its claws, you might consider having its front claws removed surgically by a vet—especially if your cat stays indoors. Most cats are still able to climb trees and hunt after this operation.

KOSHKA'S TREK

This remarkable true story of a six-year-old house cat began on a pleasant but uneventful summer vacation. Koshka and her people were driving through the mountains when she jumped out of the car. A few minutes later she found herself alone on an empty highway, her home far away. If she could tell us what happened next, this is what she might have said.

Almost immediately I knew I was in trouble. Those high mountains, all covered in dark and tangled forests, were no place for a house cat.

I plodded over to the edge of the road and jumped down onto a grassy hillside. Everything was so bewildering. Where was my family? Why did they leave me? How would I get home? After a while, however, the warm sunshine made me feel better, so I ran fast, my tail high.

Following the twisting banks of a stream, I came to a forested slope. On I tramped, under trees dressed in long green needles, and upward through leafy ferns crowding the gloomy forest floor. Finally I found myself high on a cliff overlooking a valley with purple mountains that towered over the far side. Below was a river, flashing like a silver ribbon, and a little village. Somehow, I knew that my way home lay through the valley and over the mountains.

First, though, I had to reach a narrow ledge that angled down across the cliff's face. I stretched forward and almost touched it—and then one more try and I was safely there. The cold wind brushed my fur and there was no sound as I crept cautiously on. The rock ahead looked secure as I stepped onto it....

I wailed, clawing at the air as I plunged upside down through space. Snapping my head around, I got turned over, but falling seeming to take forever—as if in a dream. I banged against another ledge and somersaulted away.

Finally, I crashed into water that felt hard as rock. It knocked the breath out of me. But, sputtering and coughing, I managed to swim. The water was so cold it burned, and by the time I reached the bank I was numb.

I dragged myself out and lay down. I hurt, but no bones were broken. When I felt better, I limped into a sunny meadow to rest a bit more. How happy I felt to be on flat ground again.

When I woke up, I saw something that sent a tingle through me. High up on a branch of a scraggly tree, with its back to me, sat a chipmunk. I may be a pampered house pet, but when I saw that chipmunk, I changed. Now I was a quick, silent hunter, gliding forward with my ears flat on my head. At the base of the tree I paused for a last, calculating look at my prey.

With a burst of power I leapt into the tree and clawed my way up. As I reached its branch, the chipmunk spotted me and jumped straight up in alarm. But when it came back down I was there, and in a single bite I ended its struggles.

Standing on that branch with my prey locked between my jaws, I took a moment to relax. Now I knew that I had a chance to make it. I had survived a fall from an impossible height into agonizingly cold water, and found food. I had become a wild cat, fit for a wild country. In the village below, I would be tame again, seeking food from the people there. But when I left the village, I knew I could throw off my tameness. The mountains beyond the valley no longer seemed so forbidding.

I descended the tree and ate my meal slowly. When I was done, I moved onward.

It took six months, but Koshka, using her homing instincts, did get home. Undoubtedly, there were many other dangers in her journey, but whenever the odds seemed too great, she somehow found the courage to take them on. By winter Koshka rejoined her family and became a house pet once again.

THE CAT SHOW

The first cat show was held in London, England's Crystal Palace in 1871. The organizer, Harrison Weir, wanted people to see all the different colors, markings and breeds of cats. Prizes were awarded to many of the 170 cats entered—with a prize even going to the fattest cat of all.

Today, cat shows are still popular. Their aim is to pick the best cats of all— the cats that come closest to meeting the standard set out for their breed. Before you rush out and enter your pet in a show, here are some pointers (from a cat's point of view) to consider.

*Yikes! Make sure I **don't** have fleas.*

Do make sure that my teeth are clean and free from tartar. And it's best not to feed me fish or other strong-smelling food just before a show.

Do have me in perfect health. In fact, in some countries, I'm not allowed to enter a show unless I am first examined by a vet right at the show hall.

72

94

63

21

PURRRFECT HEALTH

DON'T wait until the last minute to brush me. The road to cat stardom begins with regular care and grooming.

A GUIDE TO CAT SHOW TALK

If you ever visit a cat show, here are some words and terms (and their meanings) that you might hear...

Agouti: The color between a tabby's stripes. Non-agouti cats don't have this background color so their coat is all one color.

Ailurophile: A person who loves cats.

Almond: The shape of eyes in some foreign or oriental breeds.

Aoc: Any other color—any color other than those recognized specifically by the breed.

Aov: Any other variety—any pedigreed cat not specifically recognized as a member of a breed.

Balanced: A cat with good proportions in relation to the standard of points for its particular breed or variety.

Benching: Placing a cat with all its show equipment in its pen at the cat show, ready for judging.

Bicolor: A coat that is patched white and another color.

Blaze: A marking down the center of the forehead.

Bonnet Ears: Cat ears that are held sideways and forwards. A cat will sometimes hold its ears like this when it's feeling nervous.

Brush: The tail of a long-haired cat.

Butterfly: The shape of the pattern of markings on the shoulders of blotched, classic or marbled tabby cats.

Cat Fancy: A name for organized cat breeding and showing activities.

Champion (Grand Champion): Title won by cats after winning a number of special awards at cat shows.

Coarse: A cat that is larger or heavier than set out by its breed standard.

Cobby: A cat with a short, compact body with broad shoulders and rump, short tail and large, rounded head.

Conformation: The essential characteristics distinguishing a breed.

Fancier: A person who breeds or shows cats as a serious hobby.

Foreign: A cat whose body is fine-boned and elegant, as in the Siamese.

Gait: The way a cat walks or runs.

Gauntlets: The white markings on the legs of a Birman.

Ghost Markings: Faint tabby markings seen in some solid-colored cats, especially when they are young.

Gloves: The white feet as seen on Birmans.

Registration: Recording the details of a cat's birth and ancestry with an official cat organization.

Roman: A cat's nose with a high, prominent bridge, as seen in some Siamese cats.

Rosette: A rose-shaped ribbon awarded to prize-winners at cat shows.

Ruff: The fur around a long-haired cat's neck.

Rumpy: A true Manx cat with a well-rounded rump and no detectable tail structure.

Nose Leather: The smooth piece of skin between a cat's nostrils.

Hock: The ankle of a cat's hind leg.

Hot: A cream-colored cat with too much red in its coat.

Tufts: Small clusters of hairs at the tips of some cats' ears, often seen in Abyssinians.

Mask: The darker-colored areas of the face, as seen in Siamese cats.

Mayor's Chains: The lines around the neck of the classic tabby.

Muzzle: The nose and jaws of a cat.

Pencilling: The fine lines on the cheeks of tabby cats.

Points: The extremities of a cat's body—the head, ears, tail and feet—that are colored (in Siamese and some other breeds).

Pricked: Cat ears held high and alert.

SELF
SOLID

Whip: A tail that is long, thin and tapering, as seen in Siamese cats.

Self (solid): A solid-colored coat that is the same color all over.

Shading: The gradual variation in coat color, usually from the back to the belly.

Show Standard: A description of the ideal cat of a particular breed, against which real cats are judged at a cat show.

Stifle: The knee of a cat's hind leg.

TO THE VET'S

The annual check-up for your cat is a very important event, but your cat may be nervous about going, especially if it has experienced needles and bumpy car rides on past trips to the vet. You can help your cat overcome its fears by comforting and stroking it, and being happy on the way and while you are there. Some cats even purr through the whole vet visit.

And the annual check-up is a great time for you to ask all the questions about your cat that you have been saving up.

What will the vet be checking for?

Bright, clear and clean eyes are a sign your cat is feeling well.

Your cat's teeth should look clean and white, but how are its gums? They should be a solid pink color, not too pale and not bright red.

Worms? Take a specimen from the kitty litter so that your vet can check to make sure your cat does not have a worm problem.

How about ear mites or fleas? Cats can catch these and a vet is the best person to help you with this problem.

If you think your cat's heart is racing, it is. A cat's heart beats twice as fast as yours—about 110 to 140 times a minute.

Who likes a needle? But if your cat is to live a long, happy and healthy life it needs its shots. So be sure to ask your vet how your cat should be protected from infectious diseases. M-E-O-W-TCH!

CASSANDRA BECOMES A CHAMPION

This is the true story of a very special cat. It all began when Natasha and Mike Rosnok of Nova Scotia, Canada, found a stray kitten. The poor little cat was missing part of her front leg and couldn't stand, so Natasha and Mike decided to help. At first their parents said the cat must be put to sleep, but later they changed their minds. The wonderful story of what happened to the kitten is told for you here by Natasha, age 9, in her own words.

"Mike and I cried all the way to the vet's and begged Mom and Dad not to put the pussycat to sleep. We called her Cassandra. Mom finally said that if the vet could fix her up we could keep her. The vet said that he could try to save her, but he would have to amputate her leg and operate on her shoulder. Cassandra was in the hospital for a long while.

"Finally it was time for us to take Cassandra home. We fixed up a corner of the bedroom for her with a pink kitty basket and a soft white blanket. We had to watch her carefully and give her medicine for 10 days. Finally, she started to get around on her own, limping along on three legs. At first she was afraid to come out of her room. She would peek through the door and come slowly up the hall. Then she would run back into the room and hide under the bed. But soon she got used to our house and even made friends with our other cat and dog. We didn't allow her to go out in the yard alone because we were afraid that she couldn't run fast enough if a strange dog chased her. But I took her out for walks on a leash after school and she enjoyed this very much.

"One day we heard about a cat show at the Metro Centre in Halifax, Nova Scotia, Canada. I wanted to take Cassandra. We sent in her registration and everything. I started to brush her every day and get her all ready for it.

"Then one day, Mom told me I couldn't bring her to the show. The lady in charge of the show had called Mom and said that Cassandra was disqualified because she only had three legs. She said that a cat has to have two ears, two eyes, one tail and four legs to be in the show. I got really angry and I told Mom that that wasn't fair. I said 'That is discrimination. Cassandra can't help it if she has only three legs'. Then Mom said I was right. She called the lady and told her that I was very, very angry at their stupid rules. Then the lady called the bosses of the cat show. She called me back and said that they had changed their rules and Cassandra could be in the show after all.

"We got up very early in the morning to go to the show. There were about a hundred cats, in all sorts of different colors. There were four cat judges from the United States and Canada. They were judging the cats all day long. One judge gave Cassandra fifth place; one gave her second place; one gave her fifth place again; and then one gave her first place! She won 20 ribbons and four rosettes. When all the points were counted, Cassandra had won more than any cat in the show.

"She won for beauty, balance, health and cleanliness and was named the best household pet in Eastern Canada. Her big ribbon said she was 'Best of the Best!' Lots of people came to talk to me and told me that they weren't allowed to bring their cats to the show because they only had one eye or no tail. I told them how Cassandra stood up for her rights. They said they were going to bring their cats next time. They will never again be allowed to keep handicapped pussycats out of the cat show in Nova Scotia.

"One week later, a man and two ladies came to our house and gave Cassandra the Morris Award. This award is given to very important cats. We made a chocolate cake and decorated it with pink frosting and wrote, "Congratulations Cassandra" on it. Some of my friends came over to see Cassandra get her award and we had a party for her. We wrapped a can of tuna fish in birthday paper and put it next to the cake for her. Cassandra was very happy."

Tina Holdcroft

THE CAT'S MEOW

The world would certainly be a different place if it weren't for cats. And so would our language. There are 16 cat expressions hidden in this scene. How many can you find? We'll get you started by "letting the cat out of the bag."

Answers on page 96